A Treasury of
ESSENTIAL PROVERBS

A Treasury of
ESSENTIAL
PROVERBS

Collected, Arranged and
Introduced by
RODNEY DALE

◆ B O O K ◆ B L O C K S ◆

However vast the ocean, the diver's
dimensions remain unchanged

On aphorisms, maxims, proverbs, sayings and other gnomic utterances

That we are born with plenty of inbuilt automatic control of our bodies is surely in no doubt. From the moment of our emergence – all being well – we breathe, our hearts beat, we ingest, metabolise and excrete, all with no instruction at all . . . in short, our biochemical processes carry on without training or intervention. In due time, we begin to crawl without assistance; it's only when we come to experiment with walking that our parents think they're teaching us something – presumably because walking is an action they (think they) understand; in fact, the internal control processes are much more complex than the end result of balancing upright and putting one foot in front of the other might have us believe – if we think about it at all.

Less obvious, perhaps, is the process of learning to talk. Certainly being talked to (or hearing people talk) helps that process, but even this concentrates on vocabulary, with little hint of how to put the words together in one of the many possible acceptable orders.

If all that we take for granted in speech had to be taught there would be no end to the teaching – otherwise, a child would hardly be able to learn its language (as it does) by listening to the 'shape' of what others are saying. Each word would have to be explained (not only what it means but how it's used) and life ain't like that . . . hence Professor Noam Chomsky's conclusion that the biologically-based material with which we are endowed at birth includes the equipment to acquire language. Since the 'native' language one acquires might be one of hundreds, the implication is that, different as the advanced results of one's language-learning process may be, the fundamentals of all language must have something in common.

Let me illustrate our innate feeling for the 'rightness' or otherwise of language by quoting the opening (or closing) stanza of Jabberwocky:

> 'Twas brillig, and the slithy toves
> Did gyre and gimble in the wabe;
> All mimsy were the borogoves,
> And the mome raths outgrabe.

When we first heard that, presumably before encountering Carroll's interpretation that follows it, we must surely have accepted its construction without question, whatever we thought of its meaning.

Now, if I take that last sentence, and rearrange

its twenty-five words in alphabetical order (and give them a slight tweak), the result is hardly an acceptable sentence – yet our minds either see, or strive to find, meanings in pairs and groups of its words, even though we know quite well that there is (meant to be) none.

It seems to me that striving to relate any random stimulus to something one understands is an essential property of the brain – it's particularly strong on finding faces in patterns, a visual analogue of finding sense in random words. Here's the rearranged sentence:

Accepted without before Carroll's we construction encountering first have when heard we interpretation its its meaning must presumably of question surely that thought we whatever.

Having accepted the lack of meaning we find that, if we do wish to read the words out loud fluently, we have to treat them as a word list; that the 'feeling' of reading such a piece is very different from reading either sense – or nonsense – in a grammatically correct framework.

So the demonstrated result is that nonsense vocabulary in a grammatically correct framework (Jabberwocky) is more acceptable to our ears than a sequence of legitimate words without grammatical form. That in this sense the grammar 'matters' more than the words speaks much for its universal, Chomskyan, importance.

The purpose of that lengthy build-up was to explore some of the hidden and unsung properties of language so as to focus our thoughts on what might lie behind so-called gnomic utterances. I believe that another inherent property of language, and its interpretation, and what makes a given utterance acceptable (or otherwise) to us, must be our ability to immediately recognise and therefore accept allegorical statements whose function is to illustrate the generic through reference to the specific – even via some absurd statement outwith our normal experience whose interpretation emerges as nonetheless quite straightforward.

Take, for example, 'A stitch in time saves nine'. This phrase – which many people immediately call to mind when asked for a proverb – says more in its six words than might otherwise be expressed in sixty (or even six hundred). But when you utter it – as everyone does from time to time – no one turns a hair. The proverb carries with it a generic meaning that 'everybody knows', which is quite separate from its specific, literal one. That this is the case may be illustrated by the fact that, when it is uttered in a context where it does indeed refer to, say, a seam starting to come apart, it often gives rise to a knowing snigger that, on reflection, it really doesn't merit.

'A stitch in time saves nine' describes a recognisable reality. But how about 'When the owl goes to the mouse picnic, he's not there for the sack races'? Do we conjure up the scene of the incontinent little rodents, some sitting around pogged on rugs among the remains of the feast; others organising themselves into heats for the hessian hop, while all the time the visiting Old Brown puts them at their unwitting ease by nonchalantly relaxing in the grandstand behind a benign and studiedly vacuous smile? Probably not; our minds immediately identify the utterance for what it is, and leap to its generic meaning with no trouble. Moreover, if a circumstance arises in which it might be used, the mind makes its connection, and up pop the words ready for utterance.

The proverbs in this book, then, do not represent some fanciful bolt-on goodies to our phrasal vocabulary – they are part of our very make-up. We not only immediately recognise them for what they are when we see (or hear) them; we also automatically endow them with their generic (rather than their specific) meaning, and bring them out as appropriate. And further evidence of their place in our language is found in the fact that such utterances are not only found in all cultures (and hence in all languages), but that they also date from the very earliest times.

I hope the foregoing endues the following collection with even more food for thought. The proverbs are arranged in an alphabetical order based on their key words; thus some may appear more than once. And if you don't find you favourite here . . . well, you may find something better in the space that it might have occupied.

RODNEY DALE
Haddenham, Cambridgeshire
May 2003

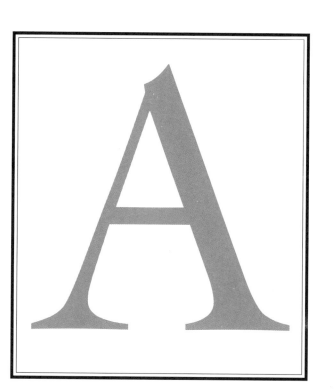

He that lies long abed, his estate feels it

Gentility without ability is worse than plain
beggary

Absence diminishes little passions and increases
great ones

Absence makes the heart grow fonder

Absence sharpens love; presence strengthens it

The absent are always in the wrong

The absent are never without fault,
nor the present without excuse

Accidents will happen in the
best regulated families

There is no good accord, where
every man would be a lord

There is no accounting for tastes

Acorns were good till bread was found

Great oaks from little acorns grow

A class act needs no cue-cards

'Tis action that makes the hero

Actions speak louder than words

As good be an addled egg as an idle bird

Adversity makes a strange bedfellow

Prosperity makes friends; adversity tries them

Advice when most needed is least heeded

A good scare is worth more than good advice

Advice is a stranger;
welcome he stays the night;
unwelcome he leaves at once

If you wish good advice, consult an old man

It is as hard to follow good
advice as to give it

❀

When a thing is done, advice comes too late

❀

Write down the advice of him who loves you,
though you like it not at present

❀

While the discreet advise,
the fool does his business

❀

Affection blinds reason

A bright morning bodes a wet afternoon

A lean agreement is better
than a fat judgement

He that buys land buys many stones;
he that buys flesh buys many bones;
He that buys eggs buys many shells; but
he that buys good ale buys nothing else

A wise man is never less alone
than when he is alone

Better be alone than in bad company

❁

St Paul's will not always stand

❁

Ambition makes people diligent

❁

Fools rush in where angels fear to tread

❁

Men are not angels

❁

Anger and haste hinder good counsel

Anger dies quickly within a good man

Anger ends in cruelty

Anger has no eyes

Anger restrained is wisdom gained

Don't let the sun go down on your anger

The anger is not warrantable
that has seen two suns

A hungry man is an angry man

He that is angry is seldom at ease

He who slowly gets angry keeps
his anger longer

He who wisdom has at will,
an angry heart can hold him still

Two things a man should never be angry at;
what he can help, and what he cannot help

When angry, count a hundred

Like question, like answer

It is better to be the hammer than the anvil

An ape's an ape, a varlet's a varlet,
though they be clad in silk or scarlet

The higher the ape goes, the more
he shows his tail

Eat an apple going to bed,
and make the doctor beg his bread

The apple never falls far from the tree

The rotten apple injures its neighbours

The ex-apprentice is still the little ol'boy

An army marches on its stomach

An arrow shot upright falls on
the shooter's head

Big arrows, small maps
That's the way to kill the chaps

❋

Art is long, life is short

❋

Authority shows the man

❋

Beware of an oak, it draws the stroke;
avoid an ash, it counts the flash;
creep under a thorn,
it can save you from harm

Ask but enough, and you may lower
the price as you list

Ask much to have a little

Ask not what boils in another's pot

Better to ask the way than go astray

Better ride on an ass that carries me
than a horse that throws me

Attack is the best form of defence

Like author, like book

If you wish to know a man,
give him authority

B

Bachelors' wives and maids' children
are well taught

Bad news travels fast

Where bad's the best, bad must be the choice

The bait hides the hook

A bare foot is better than none

At a good bargain, think twice

Why keep a dog and bark yourself?

It is an ill battle where the devil
carries the colours

Don't sell the skin till you have caught the bear

A beard well lathered is a beard half shaved

It is not the beard that makes the philosopher

If you can't beat 'em, join 'em

It is good beating proud folks,
for they'll not complain

❀

A thing of beauty is a joy for ever

❀

Beauty and honesty seldom agree

❀

Beauty is but a blossom

❀

Beauty is eloquent even when silent

❀

Beauty is in the eye of the beholder

Beauty is only one layer

❀

Beauty is potent but money is omnipotent

❀

Beauty may have fair leaves, yet bitter fruit

❀

Beauty opens locked doors

❀

Beauty won't make the pot boil

❀

Goodness is better than beauty

Health and gaiety foster beauty

❊

If Jack's in love, he's no judge of Jill's beauty

❊

As you make your bed, so you must lie in it

❊

Go to bed with the lamb and rise with the lark

❊

A swarm of bees in May is worth a load of hay

❊

Where are bees, there is honey

A beggar can never be bankrupt

Set a beggar on horseback and
he'll ride to the devil

Beggars breed and rich men feed

Beggars can't be choosers

Gentility without ability is worse
than plain beggary

Better never to begin than never to make an end

❀

A good beginning makes a good ending

❀

Everything must have a beginning

❀

Well begun is half done

❀

Belief is better than investigation

❀

Believe nothing of what you hear,
and only half of what you see

Seeing is believing

Better fill a man's belly than his eye

The belly carries the legs

Better bend than break

Best is best cheap

The best may be the enemy of the good

The best of men are but men at best

The best things in life are free

Big is beautiful

Every bullet has its billet

Fast bind, fast find

He that borrows binds himself with
his neighbour's rope

A bird in the hand is worth two in the bush

A little bird is content with a little nest

Every bird loves to hear himself sing

The early bird catches the worm

Fine feathers make fine birds

Every dog is allowed one bite

Once bitten, twice shy

Two blacks don't make a white

The blacksmith's horse is always the worst shod

He that blames would buy

If the blind lead the blind,
both shall fall into the ditch

In the country of the blind,
the one-eyed man is king

There are none so blind as those
who will not see

❀

There is no blindness like ignorance

❀

Ignorance is bliss

❀

Blood is thicker than water

❀

Good blood makes bad puddings
without groats or suet

❀

Good wine engenders good blood

A wise man needs not blush for changing
his purpose

Bold men have generous hearts

He was a bold man that first ate an oyster

Fair words break no bones

A closed book is but a block

Every book must be chewed to get out its juice

No book is a best seller before it's published

You can't judge a book by its cover

You cannot open a book without
learning something

They that are booted are not always ready

As soon as man is born he begins to die

He that trusts to borrowed ploughs,
will have his land lie fallow

The borrower is servant to the lender

He that goes a borrowing, goes a sorrowing

A drunkard's purse is his bottle

To bow the body is easy,
to bow the will is hard

Boys will be boys

Boys will be men

Great braggers, little doers

An idle brain is the devil's workshop

Where there's muck, there's brass

A brave man's wounds are seldom on his back

Better bend than break

Beware of breeding

You can't make bricks without straw

Every bride is a great beauty

Don't cross a bridge until you come to it

A briefcase may contain but sandwiches

If it ain't broke don't fix it

A new broom sweeps clean

Building and borrowing,
a sack full of sorrowing

Building and marrying of children
are great wasters

No good building without a good foundation

It is not the burden, but the over-burden
that kills the beast

Good wine needs no bush

Busiest men find the most leisure time

Drive your business, do not let it drive you

Every man knows his own business best

Who has no haste in his business,
mountains to him seem valleys

He that is busy, is tempted by but one devil;
he that is idle, by a legion

To get it done, ask a busy man

Who is more busy, than he that has least to do?

They that have got good store of butter
may lay it thick on their bread

The buyer needs a hundred eyes,
the seller but one

There are more foolish buyers
than foolish sellers

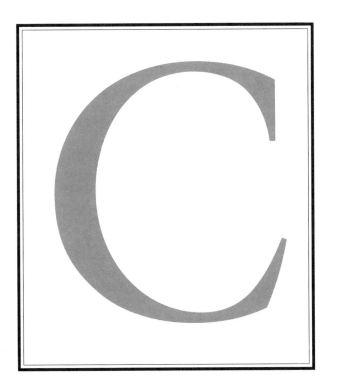

If only I had a filing cabinet I could be tidy

Caesar's wife must be above suspicion

You can't have your cake and eat it

Don't eat the calf in the cow's belly

They won't call back; you'll have to ring again

The camel never sees its own hump, but that
of its brother is always before its eyes

He can who believes he can

✤

There is no pack of cards without a knave

✤

A pound of care will not pay an ounce of debt

✤

Two cars don't go twice as fast

✤

Well goes the case when wisdom counsels

✤

A cat may look at a king

Cats hide their claws

When the cat's away, the mice will play

All cats are grey in the dark

You never get a second chance
to make a first impression

A change is as good as a rest

Change your dwelling-place often, for the
sweetness of life consists in variety

The more it changes,
the more it remains the same

Charity begins at home

Charon waits for all

Good cheap is dear

Nothing's cheap when you see it sold

Don't count your chickens
before they are hatched

A little child weighs on your knee,
a big one on your heart

The child is father of the man

The child says nothing, but what it
heard by the fire

The first service a child does
his father is to make him foolish

Children and fools must
not play with edged tools

Children are poor men's riches

Children pick up words as pigeons do peas,
and utter them again as God shall please

Children should be seen and not heard

He that has no children brings them up well

When children stand quiet,
they have done some ill

If you can't ride two horses at once,
you shouldn't be in the circus

Civility costs nothing

Cleanliness is next to godliness

Even clever men talk nonsense

Hasty climbers have sudden falls

One cannot put back the clock

From clogs to clogs is only three generations

Good clothes open all doors

Every cloud has a silver lining

He that pries into every cloud may be
stricken with a thunderbolt

Ne'er cast a clout till May is out

Scratch a clown and find a Hamlet

Let the cobbler stick to his last

Every cock crows on his own dunghill

He is not fit to command others,
that cannot command himself

Good company upon the road is
the shortest cut

It is good to have company in trouble

The company makes the feast

Conscience doth make cowards of us all

Men whose consciences are clear,
of a knock at midnight have no fear

A guilty conscience needs no accuser

Too much consulting confounds

Content is the philosopher's stone,
that turns all it touches into gold

Too many cooks spoil the broth

A good word costs no more than a bad one

Content lodges oftener in the cottage
than in the palace

Counsel is irksome when the matter
is past remedy

Counsel must be followed, not praised

Counsels in wine seldom prosper

Give neither counsel nor salt till
you are asked for it

If the counsel be good,
no matter who gave it

The counsel thou wouldst have
another keep, first keep it thyself

The land is never void of counsellors

Count to ten; breathe again

❀

So many countries, so many customs

❀

Courtesy is the inseparable
companion of virtue

❀

You can't judge a book by its cover

❀

Every ambitious man is a captive and
every covetous one a pauper

The cow knows not what her tail is
worth till she has lost it

Conscience doth make cowards of us all

It is better to be a coward for a minute
than dead for the rest of your life

Put a coward to his mettle and
he'll fight the devil

The cowl does not make the monk

You cannot make a crab walk straight

What's learnt in the cradle lasts till the tomb

Creditors have better memories than debtors

Two's company, three's a crowd

Cruelty is the strength of the wicked

Don't cry before you are hurt

Don't cry stinking fish

There's many a slip 'twixt cup and lip

What can't be cured must be endured

Curiosity is ill manners
in another's house

Curiosity is endless, restless, and useless

Curses, like chickens, come home to roost

Custom is the plague of wise men,
and the idol of fools

The customer is always right

Fear can keep a man out of danger,
but courage can support him in it

The darkest hour is that before the dawn

A light-heeled mother makes
a heavy-heeled daughter

A son is a son till he gets him a wife, but a
daughter's a daughter all the days of her life

He who works before dawn will
soon be his own master

There's nothing so dead as a
solved crossword clue

There are none so deaf as those
who will not hear

A thing you don't want is dear at any price

The dearer it is the cheaper

Death keeps no calendar

Death pays all debts

Death is the poor man's best physician

Fear of death is worse than death itself

Debt is the worst poverty

A pound of care will not pay an ounce of debt

Better to pay and have little
than have much and be in debt

Debt is an evil conscience

Deceivers have full mouths
and empty hands

A man of words and not of deeds
is like a garden full of weeds

Words are mere bubbles of water
but deeds are drops of gold

Delay is the antidote of anger

We soon believe what we desire

He is a fool that despises a child's service

Better the devil you know than
the saint you don't

Cruelty is the first attribute of the devil

Give the devil his due

He that serves God for money,
will serve the devil for better wages

He that sups with the devil
needs a long spoon

❀

If it rains when the sun is shining,
the devil is beating his wife

❀

If the devil find a man idle,
he'll set him to work

❀

Needs must when the devil drives

❀

The devil can quote scripture
for his own purpose

The devil makes his Christmas-pies of lawyer's
tongues and clerk's fingers

Wickedness with beauty is the
devil's hook baited

Ignorance is the mother of devotion

Better die with honour than
live with the shame

Diligence is the mother of good fortune

For the diligent the week has seven todays;
for the slothful seven tomorrows

If you want your dinner,
don't offend the cook

It's hard to lose a sense of direction
you've never had

Fling enough dirt and some will stick

We must eat a peck of dirt before we die

A man's discontent is his worst evil

❁

Discretion is the better part of valour

❁

Distance lends enchantment to the view

❁

Murder often: divorce N E V E R!

❁

Do as you would be done by

❁

Those who can, do; those who can't, teach

An apple a day keeps the doctor away

Evil doers are evil dreaders

Great braggers, little doers

He that does what he should not,
shall feel what he would not

A dog with two tails may turn
out to have no head

Cut off a dog's tail and he will be a dog still

❀

Double the length of its leash, and a dog
can bite four times as many people

❀

Every dog is a lion at home

❀

If the dog is not at home, he barks not

❀

You can't teach an old dog new tricks

❀

It is profound ignorance that
inspires the dogmatic tone

Doing is better than saying

❀

Doubt is the key of knowledge

❀

He that knows nothing, doubts nothing

❀

He who drinks a little too much
drinks much too much

Constant dripping wears away the stone

❀

Easy to drown in a pond as in an ocean

A drunkard's purse is his bottle

Drink only with the duck

A dwarf on a giant's shoulders
sees the further of the two

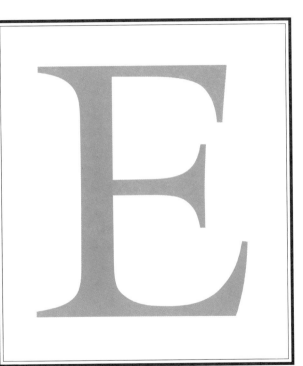

Eagles do not breed doves

Early to bed and early to rise, makes a man
healthy, wealthy, and wise

In vain they rise early that used to rise late

The early man never borrows
from the late man

Little pitchers have big ears

Easier said than done

That which is easily done, is soon believed

Easter so longed for is gone in a day

Easy come, easy go

Eat to live; don't live to eat

Often and little eating makes a man fat

Education polishes good natures
and correcteth bad ones

A black hen may lay a white egg

Better an egg today than a hen tomorrow

Don't put all your eggs in one basket

Don't teach your grandmother
to suck eggs

You can't make an omelette
without breaking eggs

Elbow grease gives the best polish

Touch not your eye
but with your elbow

An elephant never forgets

Give him an inch and he'll take a mile

Beauty is eloquent even when silent

Better go to heaven in rags
than to hell in embroidery

Better never to begin than never
to make an end

He who wills the end, wills the means

The end justifies the means

He conquers who endures

An enemy may chance to give good counsel

An enemy to beauty is a foe to nature

Art has no enemy but ignorance

Believe no tales from an enemy's tongue

For a flying enemy make a golden bridge

Make your enemy your friend

One enemy can do more hurt than
ten friends can do good

There is no little enemy

Though thine enemy seem a mouse,
watch him like a lion

❀

Enough is enough

❀

Speak to the engineer, not his sweat-rag

❀

An Englishman's home is his castle

❀

Enough is as good as a feast

❀

He who envies admits his inferiority

An envious man waxes lean with
the fatness of his neighbour

Envy and covetousness are never satisfied

Envy eats nothing but its own heart

Envy shoots at others and wounds herself

If envy were a fever, all mankind would be ill

Nothing sharpens sight like envy

In an ermine spots are soon discovered

❀

To err is human, to forgive divine

❀

A gentleman without an estate is like
a pudding without suet

❀

Every little helps

❀

Every man bastes the fat hog

Every man for himself,
and the devil take the hindmost

Every man has his faults

Covetousness is the root of all evil

He that does evil, never weens good

Money is the root of all evil

Never do evil that good may come of it

The evil that men do lives after them,
the good is oft interrèd with their bones

The exception proves the rule

Expectation is better than realization

Many things lawful are not expedient

Experience is the mother of wisdom

Experience is the teacher of fools

Experience without learning is better than
learning without experience

❀

Trouble brings experience and
experience brings wisdom

❀

An eye for an eye, and a tooth for a tooth

❀

Better fill a man's belly than his eye

❀

Far from eye, far from heart

It is easier for a camel to go through the eye
of a needle than for a rich man to enter
into the kingdom of God

One eye of the master sees more
than ten of the servants

Please your eye and plague your heart

The eye is bigger than the belly

The eye of the master will do more
work than both of his hands

What the eye doesn't see,
the heart doesn't grieve over

Make sure that the server's eyes are
not bigger than your stomach

A fair face cannot have a crabbed heart

A good face is a letter of recommendation

Don't cut off your nose to spite your face

Good face: good fortune

He that looks in a man's face knows not
what money is in his purse

The face is no index to the heart

He that asks faintly begs a denial

Fair is not fair, but that which pleases

The fairer the paper, the fouler the blot

The fairest flowers soonest fade
The fairest silk is soonest stained

The owl thinks her own young fairest

Faith will move mountains

Men have greater faith in those things
which they do not understand

A stumble may prevent a fall

Good fame is better than a good face

Familiarity breeds contempt

Far folk fare best

Fair fowls have fair feathers

Far from home, near thy harm

Better be out of the world than
out of the fashion

Fools may invent fashions that
wise men will wear

Far behind must follow the faster

The opera isn't over till
the fat lady sings

Fate leads the willing but drives the stubborn

As a father's goodness is higher
than the mountains, so is a mother's
deeper than the sea

Like father, like son

One father is enough to govern one hundred
sons, but not a hundred sons one father

The child is father of the man

He that commits a fault, thinks
everyone speaks of it

❀

He that seeks a horse or a wife without
fault has neither steed in his stable
nor angel in his bed

❀

If you can't understand what I'm saying,
the fault is mine, not thine

❀

He is lifeless that is faultless

❀

People's faults are not written
on their foreheads

The faulty stands on his guard

A guilty conscience feels continual fear

He that hopes not for good, fears not evil

Birds of a feather flock together

He that eats the king's goose shall be
choked with the feathers

Fine feathers make fine birds

A lazy clerk deserves but a lean fee

The female of the species is more
deadlier than the male

The grass is always greener on
the other side of the fence

Festina lente

Feed a cold and starve a fever

The older the fiddle, the sweeter the tune

Every fight has its shadow

He that fights and runs away may live
to fight another day

Nature and the sin of Adam can
ill be concealed by fig-leaves

Everything new is fine

Fine dressing is a foul house swept
before the doors

The moving finger writes and, having writ
Moves on. Nor all your piety nor wit
Can call it back to cancel half a line
Nor all your tears wash out a word of it

Fingers were made before forks and
hands before knives

Fight fire with fire

Fire that's closest kept burns most of all

❀

If you play with fire, you get burnt

❀

First come, first served

❀

First impressions are the most lasting

❀

First things first

❀

He that comes first to the hill,
may sit where he will

He that rises first, is first dressed

Take the first advice of a woman
and not the second

The first blow is half the battle

All's fish that comes to the net

Don't bargain for fish that are
still in the water

Gut no fish till you get them

That fish will soon be caught
that nibbles at every bait

The best fish swim near the bottom

Mere wishes are silly fishes

The fitter is like to the sire and dam

There is no such flatterer as a man's self

Fire cannot be hidden in flax

If you lie with dogs you'll get up with fleas

The dog that is idle barks at his fleas,
but he that is hunting feels them not

A meal without flesh is
like feeding on grass

He that buys land buys many stones;
he that buys flesh buys many bones;
he that buys eggs buys many shells; but
he that buys good ale buys nothing else

He that never ate flesh,
thinks a pudding a dainty

The spirit is willing but the flesh is weak

Laws catch flies but let hornets go free
After your fling, watch for the sting

In the coldest flint there is hot fire

How can the foal amble if the
horse and mare trot?

A secret foe gives a sudden blow

Anger begins with folly,
and ends with repentance

The first degree of folly is to hold
oneself wise, the second to profess it,
the third to despise counsel

Better to eat the food than read the menu

❀

A fool may give a wise man counsel

❀

A wise man sometimes changes
his mind, a fool never

❀

A wise man may sometimes play the fool

❀

He that is born a fool is never cured

❀

What the fool does in the end,
the wise man does in the beginning

You may fool all of the people some of the time,
some of the people all of the time,
but not all of the people all of the time

From a foolish judge, a quick sentence

Fools build houses; wise men buy them

If fools went not to market,
bad wares would not be sold

Wise men have their mouth in their heart,
fools have their heart in their mouth

Zeal is fit only for wise men,
but is found mostly in fools

Footprints on the sands of time
are not made by sitting down

Forbid a thing, and that women will do

Forbidden fruit is the sweetest
There is great force hidden in a sweet command

A man apt to promise is apt to forget

Forgive and forget

The persuasion of the fortunate
sways the doubtful

Fortune favours the bold

He gains enough whom fortune loses

He that has no ill fortune,
is troubled with good

If you can go in forwards,
you can come out backwards

fine dressing is a foul house
swept before the doors

No good building without
a good foundation

Count not four, except you
have them in a wallet

The fowler's pipe sounds sweet
till the bird is caught

An old fox is not easily snared

If you deal with a fox, think of his tricks

The fox preys farthest from his home

The sleepy fox has seldom
feathered breakfasts

Though the fox run, the chicken has wings

When the fox tears open your dustbin bag,
he's not looking for caviar

Frost and fraud both end in foul

There's no such thing as a free lunch

A friend in need is a friend indeed

Speak well of your friend,
of your enemy say nothing

When I lent, I was a friend;
and when I asked, I was unkind

A man is known by his friends

Friends agree best at distance

Little intermeddling makes good friends

The best of friends must part

The frog cannot out of her bog

A tree oft transplanted bears little fruit

Love is the fruit of idleness

He who has the frying-pan
in his hand turns it at will

Patience provoked turns to fury

Nothing ventured nothing gained

He gains enough whom fortune loses

Old chains gall less than new

He that gapes until he be fed,
well may he gape until he be dead

Garlic makes a man wink, drink, and stink

Borrowed garments never fit well

He that will not go over the stile must be
thrust through the gate

He that gazes upon the sun,
shall at last be blind

He is the best general who
makes the fewest mistakes

It takes three generations to make a gentleman

Gentility without ability is
worse than plain beggary

A gentleman will do like a gentleman

He is a gentleman that has gentle conditions

Jack would be a gentleman if he had money

He who gets does much,
but he who keeps does more

A dwarf on a giant's shoulders
sees further of the two

Who receives a gift, sells his liberty

Gifts blind the eyes

Nobody ever cured a sore throat
by thinking of the giraffe

Better give a shilling than lend
half a crown and lose it

Who gives to all, denies all

People who live in glass houses
shouldn't throw stones

The first glass for thirst, the second for
nourishment, the third for pleasure,
and the fourth for madness

All that glisters is not gold

When the glow-worm lights her lamp,
then the air is always damp

A lazy ox is little better for the goad

The goat must browse where she is tied

God made the country, and
man made the town

God sends meat and the devil sends cooks

The gods send nuts to those who have no teeth

A ton of gold will not buy a second of time

Gold dust blinds all eyes

Gold is but muck

Law is a flag, and gold is the wind
that makes it wave

Liberty is more worth than gold

Look to a gown of gold, and you
will at least get a sleeve of it

The streets of London are paved with gold

When we have gold, we are in fear;
when we have none we are in danger

❀

Win gold and wear gold

❀

A golden handshake is better than ten witnesses

❀

A golden key opens every door

❀

We must not look for a golden life in an iron age

❀

All things in their being are good for something

He who does no good, does evil enough

No man better knows what good is
than he who has endured evil

As a father's goodness is higher than
the mountains, so is a mother's
deeper than the sea

To see a man do a good deed is to
forget all his faults

Goodness is better than beauty

A man has no more goods than
he gets good of

A man may lose his goods for
want of demanding them

All good things must come to an end

He that eats the king's goose
shall be choked with the feathers

What is sauce for the goose is
sauce for the gander

Wrong laws make short governance

The gown is his that wears it,
and the world his that enjoys it

Grace will last, beauty will blast

While the grass grows the horses starve

They that hold the greatest farms
pay the least rent

Beware of Greeks bearing gifts

All griefs with bread are less

All's grist that comes to the mill

Where grooms and householders are all
alike great, very disastrous will it be
for the houses and all that dwell in them

Every one is held to be innocent until
he is proven guilty

He is guilty who is not at home

The gull comes against the rain

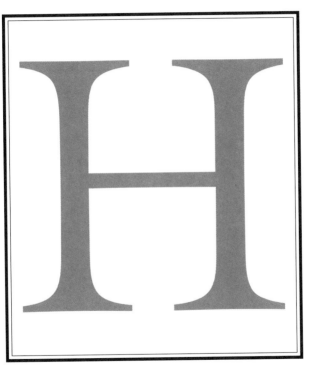

A holy habit cleanses not a foul soul

Hail brings frost in the tail

He that dwells next door to
a cripple will learn to halt

It is better to be the hammer than the anvil

The hand that rocks the cradle rules the world

Whatever is made by the hand of man, by the
hand of man may be overturned

Cold hands, warm heart

❀

Many hands make light work

❀

Handsome is as handsome does

❀

Happiness is not a horse to be harnessed

❀

Better be happy than wise

❀

Happy is the wooing that is not long a-doing

You cannot run with the hare and
hunt with the hounds

✤

If you run after two hares you will catch neither

✤

Anger and haste hinder good counsel

✤

More haste, less speed

✤

Patience is the key of joy,
but haste is the key of sorrow

✤

He that mischief hatches mischief catches

A woman either loves or hates in extremes

The love of the wicked is more dangerous
than their hatred

A still tongue makes a wise head

It is a sound head that has not a soft piece in it

Two heads are better than one

He who has good health is young;
and he is rich who owes nothing

Health is better than wealth,
especially if it eludes you

Little labour, much health

Hear all, see all, and say nothing

A blithe heart makes a blooming visage

A bold heart is half the battle

Faint heart ne'er won fair lady

Far from eye, far from heart

❀

He who opens his heart to
ambition closes it to repose

❀

Home is where the heart is

❀

Many a heart is caught in the rebound

❀

The joy of the heart makes the face fair

❀

The way to an Englishman's heart is
through his stomach

The weapon of the brave is in his heart

What the eye doesn't see, the heart
doesn't grieve over

When a heart is a fire, some sparks
will fly out of the mouth

Who has not a heart, let him have legs

If you can't stand the heat, get out of the kitchen

A hedge between keeps friendship green

Take heed of the wrath of a mighty man,
and the tumult of the people

A wicked man is his own hell

The road to hell is paved with good intentions

A little help is worth a deal of pity

The egg shows the hen the place
where to hatch

Better say 'here it is', than 'here it was'

Hew not too high lest the chips fall in thine eye

High places have their precipices

Do on the hill as you would do in the hall

Hitch your wagon to a star

Hold fast to the words of your ancestors

There's no place like home

Even Homer sometimes nods

He is wise that is honest

You cannot make people honest
by Act of Parliament

Honesty is the best policy

He that steals honey should be
aware of the sting

There is honour among thieves

Who that in youth no virtue uses,
in age all honour him refuses

Hope springs eternal in the human breast

He that hopes not for good, fears not evil

An ox is taken by its horns,
a man by his words

A horse that will not carry a saddle
deserves no oats

A running horse is an open grave

Better ride on an ass that carries me
than a horse that throws me

The best horse needs breaking,
and the aptest child needs teaching

You can take a horse to water,
but you can't make him drink

Don't change horses in midstream

If you can't ride two horses at once,
you shouldn't be in the circus

A house divided against itself cannot stand

When house and land are gone and
spent, then learning is most excellent

Humble hearts have humble desires

They must hunger in frost that
will not work in heat

A hungry man is an angry man

❀

He that hurts another hurts himself

❀

Husband makes a good wife

❀

A poor beauty finds more lovers
than husbands

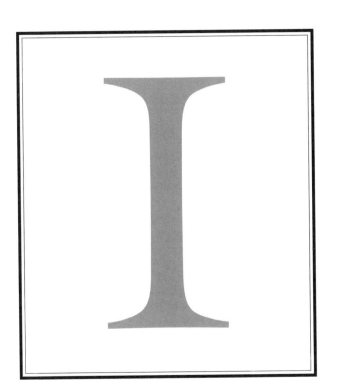

An idle youth, a needy age

❀

As good be an addled egg as an idle bird

❀

He that is busy, is tempted by but one devil;
he that is idle, by a legion

❀

Idle folks lack no excuses

❀

Idleness is the root of all evil

❀

Idleness turns the edge of wit

Of idleness comes no goodness

Ignorance and incuriosity are
two very soft pillows

Ignorance is the mother of devotion

Ignorance is the night of the mind

Ignorance is the peace of life

Ignorance of the law excuses no man

It is profound ignorance that inspires
the dogmatic tone

Where ignorance is bliss, 'tis folly to be wise

An ill life, an ill end

Better suffer ill than do ill

Fig. S1

He that does ill, hates the light

He that lives ill, fears follow him

Ill comes in by ells, and goes out by inches

Ill comes often on the back of worse

It is an ill sign to see a fox lick a lamb

Of one ill come many

Show a good man his error,
and he turns it to a virtue;
show an ill, and it doubles his fault

They that think none ill, are soonest beguiled

Imitation is the sincerest form of flattery

No one is bound to do impossibilities

Better a mischief than an inconvenience

Ignorance and incuriosity are
two very soft pillows

No man is infallible

Injuries are written in brass

Innocence is no protection

Every one is held to be innocent
until he is proven guilty

The wise forget insults,
as the ungrateful a kindness

The good intention excuses the bad action

Try to be ironic, and all too many
people will take you seriously

It is not what is he, but what has he

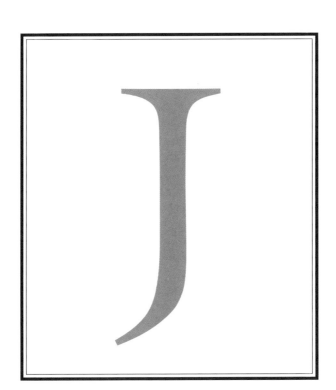

Every Jack has his Jill

Don't blame the jelly for quivering

Liberty is a jewel

None can guess the jewel by the casket

Don't blame the jigsaw piece for not fitting

If you can't beat 'em, join 'em

A rich man's jokes are always funny

A thing of beauty is a joy for ever

A good judge conceives quickly,
and judges slowly

Don't judge a book by its cover

A lean agreement is better than
a fat judgement

Much law, but little justice

Weigh justly and sell dearly

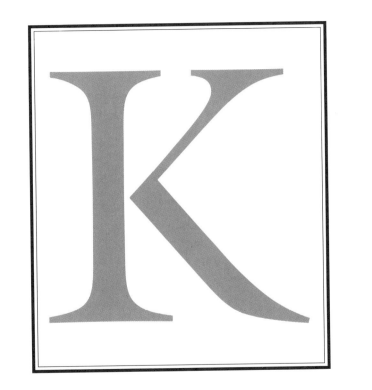

Better keep now than seek anon

He who gets does much, but he
who keeps does more

Doubt is the key of knowledge

It is not work that kills, but worry

You've got to be cruel to be kind

As fire is kindled by bellows,
so is anger by words

Kindness is lost that's bestowed
on children and old folk

❀

Every man is a king in his home

❀

Woe to the kingdom whose king is a child

❀

An apple-pie without some cheese
is like a kiss without a squeeze

❀

No knave to the learned knave

❀

Once a knave, always a knave

The more knave, the better luck

The king can make a knight,
but not a gentleman

Learn not and know not

What you don't know can't hurt you

Knowledge is no burthen

Knowledge has bitter roots but sweet fruits

Knowledge is a wild thing and
must be hunted before it can be tamed

Knowledge is folly, except grace guide it

Knowledge without practice makes
but half an artist

He that knows little, often repeats it

He that knows nothing, doubts nothing

The more one knows, the less one believes

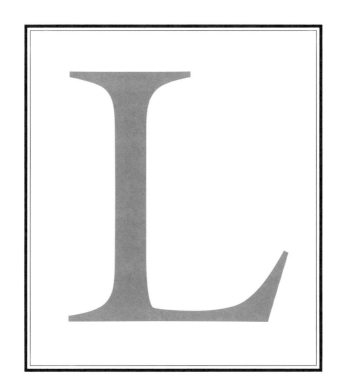

He that will not endure labour
in this world, let him not be born

Little labour, much health

If the lad go the well against his will,
either the can will break or the water will spill

No larder but has its mice

He that comes last to the pot, is soonest wroth

He that pays last never pays twice

Better late than never

He who laughs last, laughs longest

A pennyweight of love is worth
a pound of law

Every law has its loophole

In a thousand pounds of law,
there's not an ounce of love

Law governs man, reason the law

Law is a bottomless pit

Much law, but little justice

One suit of law breeds twenty

The law does not concern itself about trifles

The law grows of sin, and chastises it

Good laws often proceed from bad manners

Many lords, many laws

The more laws, the more offenders

Win your lawsuit and lose your money

Lawsuits consume time, and money,
and rest, and friends

A good lawyer makes an evil neighbour

He that is his own lawyer has a fool for a client

Laziness goes so slowly that
poverty overtakes it

A lazy ox is little better for the goad

A lazy sheep thinks its wool heavy

Learn not and know not

Learn young, learn fair

A handful of good life is better
than a bushel of learning

185

A little learning is a dangerous thing

Experience without learning is better
than learning without experience

Learning in one's youth is engraving in stone

Learning is the eye of the mind

Learning makes a man fit company for himself

Learning without wisdom is a load
of books on an ass's back

The love of money and the love
of learning rarely meet

He that nothing questions, nothing learns

Double the length of its leash, and
a dog can bite four times as many people

He that eats least eats most

The least boy always carries the greatest fiddle

They can do least who boast loudest

Raw leather will stretch

❀

Lend never that thing thou needest most

❀

Lend only that which you can afford to lose

❀

Lend sitting and you will run to collect

❀

Lend, and lose the loan, or gain an enemy

❀

Neither a borrower nor a lender be

He has but a short Lent, that must
pay money at Easter

The leopard cannot change his spots

A liar can go round the world,
but can never come back

A liar needs a good memory

The liar is sooner caught than the cripple

Liberty is a jewel

Liberty is more worth than gold

Who loses his liberty loses all

Lice do not bite busy men

As a tree fails, so shall it lie

Better a lie that heals than
a truth that wounds

Ask no questions; be told no lies

Art is long, life is short

Life begins at forty

Life is a pilgrimage

Life is half spent before we know what it is

Life is not all beer and skittles

Life is short and time is swift

Life is sweet

Life means strife

Life would be too smooth,
if it had no rubs in it

Long life has long misery

Light cheap, ether yield

Lightning never strikes twice
in the same place

Like it or lump it

Likely lies in the mire,
and unlikely gets over

Likeness causes liking

Lime makes a rich father and a poor son

Don't wash your dirty linen in public

An army of stags led by a lion would be
more formidable than one of lions led by a stag

Better be the head of a dog
than the tail of a lion

Every dog is a lion at home

Every man is a lion in his own cause

Listeners never hear good of themselves

Literature is a good staff but a bad crutch
Ask much to have a little

If you would live for ever,
you must wash milk from your liver

Live and let live

All lay loads on a willing horse

Half a loaf is better than no bread

A borrowed loan should come laughing home

Give a loan and buy a quarrel

No lock will hold against the power of gold

A crooked log may make a straight fire

Long foretold, long last;
short notice, soon past

They who live longest, will see most

Look before you leap

An ox, when he is loose,
licks himself at pleasure

A man has choice to begin love,
but not to end it

A mother's love never ages

Absence sharpens love,
presence strengthens it

All the world loves a lover

All's fair in love and war

As good love comes as goes

Calf love, half love; old love, cold love

Cold pudding will settle your love

Congruity is the mother of love

Faithfulness is a sister of love

Faults are thick where love is thin

Fear is stronger than love

Follow love and it will flee thee:
flee love and it will follow thee

Hot love, hasty vengeance

If Jack's in love, he's no judge of Jill's beauty

In a thousand pounds of law,
there's not an ounce of love

It is best to be off with the old love
before you are on with the new

Labour is light where love doth pay

Love and business teach eloquence

Love and lordship like no fellowship

Love asks faith, and faith asks firmness

Love covers many infirmities

Love is a game in which both
players always cheat

Love is a sweet torment

Love is as strong as death

Love is blind

Love is full of fear

Love is never without jealousy

Love is sweet in the beginning
but sour in the ending,

Love is the fruit of idleness

Love is the touchstone of virtue

Love is the true reward of love

Love is without reason

Love lives in cottages as well as in courts

Love makes all men equal

Love makes one fit for any work

Love makes the world go round

Love me love my dog

Love rules his kingdom without a sword

Love speaks, even when the lips are closed

Love the babe for her that bare it

Love without return is like
a question without an answer

No herb will cure love

No love is foul, nor prison fair

No love like the first love

Old love does not rust

Old love will not be forgotten

One love expels another

Perfect love casteth out fear

Salt water and absence wash away love

205

Sound love is not soon forgotten

The course of true love never did run smooth

The love of money and the love of
learning rarely meet

The love of money is the root of all evil

The love of the wicked is more
dangerous than their hatred

They love too much that die for love

True love never grows old

When love is greatest, words are fewest

When love puts in, friendship is gone

Where love is, there is faith

Where there is no trust there is no love

Whom the gods love dies young

Whom we love best, to them we can say least

Write down the advice of him who loves you,
though you like it not at present

Men are best loved furthest off

A poor beauty finds more
lovers than husbands

There is more pleasure in loving
than in being beloved

Loyalty is worth more than money

Care and diligence bring luck

Ill luck is good for something

What is worse than ill luck?

Late was often lucky

The more wicked, the more lucky

Beauty's sister is vanity,
and her daughter lust

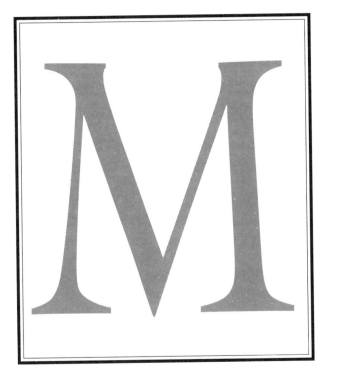

Where MacGregor sits is the head of the table

A maid that laughs is half taken

A maiden with many wooers
often chooses the worst

All are not maidens that wear bare hair

A man at five may be a fool at fifteen

A man is as old as the woman he feels

A man is known by his friends

A man is known by the company he keeps

A man is valued as he makes himself valuable

A man may woo where he will, but will
wed where his hap is

A man must plough with such oxen as he has

A man must sell his ware after
the rates of the market

A man of courage never wants weapons

God made man, man made money

God made the country, and man made the town

Man proposes; God disposes

The healthful man can give counsel to the sick

Whatever man has done, man may do

Wherever a man dwell, he shall be sure to
have a thorn-bush near his door

❀

A dog in a manger soon needs new straw

❀

Manners and money make a gentleman

❀

Manners make often fortunes

❀

Nurture and good manners maketh man

❀

He threatens many that hurts any

Big arrows, small maps,
that's the way to kill the chaps

March winds and April showers
bring forth May flowers

Buy in the cheapest market and
sell in the dearest

Marriages are made in heaven

Where every man is master,
the world goes to wrack

A good maxim is never out of season

⚜

Ne'er cast a clout till May is out

⚜

Meat and mass never hindered any man

⚜

Meat is much, but manners is more

⚜

Meddle not with another man's matter

⚜

A liar needs a good memory

A man of great memory without learning,
has a rock and a spindle,
and no stuff to spin

❀

All men are mortal

❀

Boys will be men

❀

Do as men do, then most men
will speak well of you

❀

Keep good men company and
you shall be of their number

Least said, soonest mended

Better to eat the food than read the menu

A merchant that gains not, loses

He that could know what would be dear,
need be a merchant but one year

An ounce of vanity spoils
a hundredweight of merit

All are not merry that dance lightly

Mettle is dangerous in a blind horse

God gives the milk but not the pail

It's no use crying over spilt milk

Wine is old men's milk

You cannot sell the cow and sup the milk

Little things please little minds

What's yours is mine and
what's mine is my own

There are more miracles in a cask of wine
than in a church full of saints

Mischief comes by the pound and
goes away by the ounce

Mischief comes without calling for

Our worst misfortunes are those
which never befall us

It is easy to bear the misfortunes of others

Misfortune arrives on horseback
but departs on foot

Misfortune is not that which can be avoided,
but that which cannot

Misfortunes find their way even
on the darkest night

Misfortunes tell us what fortune is

A miss is as good as a mile

When the mist comes from the hill,
then good weather it doth spill;
When the mist comes from the sea,
then good weather it will be

Modesty sets off one newly come to honour

Though modesty be a virtue,
yet bashfulness is a vice

Monday's child is fair of face,
Tuesday's child is full of grace;
Wednesday's child is full of woe,
Thursday's child has far to go;
Friday's child is loving and giving,
Saturday's child works hard for its living;
and the child that's born on the Sabbath day,
is fair and wise and good and gay

He that has money has what he wants

If you would know what money is,
go borrow some

Money governs the world

Money is often lost for want of money

Money is the only monarch

Money is the sinews of love as well as of war

Money isn't everything

Money makes a man free everywhere

Money makes money

Much money makes a country poor,
for it sets a dearer price on everything

Of money, wit, and virtue,
believe one-fourth of what you hear

Ready money is a ready medicine

Want of money, want of comfort

When money speaks, the world is silent

Will buys and money pays

A moneyless man goes fast
through the market

Speak to the organ-grinder, not his monkey

The full moon brings fair weather

A bright morning bodes a wet afternoon

An hour in the morning is
worth two in the evening

Red sky at night, shepherd's delight;
Red sky in the morning, shepherd's warning

The morning sun never lasts a day

All men are mortal

As a father's goodness is higher
than the mountains,
so is a mother's deeper than the sea

A light-heeled mother makes
a heavy-heeled daughter

A man's mother is his other God

A mother's love never ages

An ounce of mother is
worth a ton of priest

It is not as thy mother says,
but as thy neighbours say

Like mother, like daughter

The good mother says not 'Will you?' but gives

The mother's breath is aye sweet

The mother's side is the surest side

Don't make a mountain out of a molehill

If the mountain will not go to Mahomet,
Mahomet must go to the mountain

The higher the mountain the greater descent

It is a bold mouse that breeds in the cat's ear

Well kens the mouse when the
cat's out of the house

What is sweet in the mouth is oft
bitter in the stomach

Mastery mows the meadows down

Muck and money go together

Where there's muck there's brass

Murder often: divorce N E V E R!

Murder will out

Women and music should never be dated

What must be must be

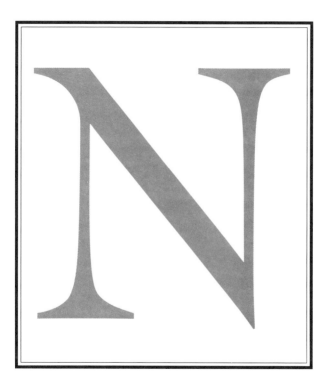

Need makes the naked man run

Nature and the sin of Adam can
ill be concealed by fig-leaves

Nature hates all sudden changes

Nature, time, and patience
are the three great physicians

Nurture is above nature

You can drive out Nature with a pitchfork,
but she keeps on coming back

An idle youth, a needy age

It is not as thy mother says,
but as thy neighbours say

He has ill neighbours,
that is fain to praise himself

A little bird is content with a little nest

Never answer a question until it is asked

Never be boastful;
someone may pass who knew you as a child

Never be wary of well doing

Never cheapen unless you mean to buy

Never do evil that good may come of it

Never do things by halves

Never judge by appearances

Never look a gift horse in the mouth

Never open the door to a little vice,
lest a great one enter with it

Never open your pack, and sell no wares

Never refuse a good offer

Never return to the restaurant
where you had that excellent meal

Never spend your money before you have it

Never was a scornful person well-received

Never were the absent in the right

What you've never had you never miss

Everything new is fine

New lords, new laws

❀

New meat begets a new appetite

❀

New things are fair

❀

What is new cannot be true

❀

Night is the mother of counsel

❀

'No, thank you' has lost many
a good butter-cake

Don't say 'No' till you are asked

If you always say 'No', you'll never be married

Nobility, without ability, is like a pudding
wanting suet

He is noble that has noble conditions

The more noble, the more humble

Blessèd is he who expecteth nothing,
for he shall not be disappointed

By doing nothing we learn to do ill

He that does nothing, does ever amiss

He that has nothing need fear to lose nothing

Nothing is certain but death and taxes

Nothing is certain but the unforeseen

Nothing is given so freely as advice

Nothing is impossible to a willing heart

Nothing seek, nothing find

Nothing so good but it might
have been better

Nothing's cheap when you see it sold

Where nothing is, a little does ease

Good words cost nought

There comes nought out
of the sack but what
was there

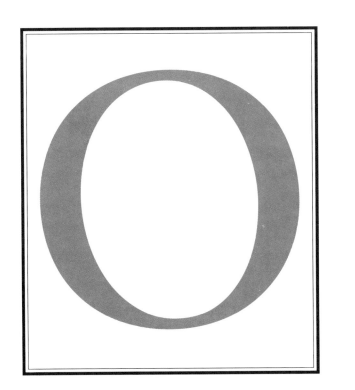

An oak is not felled at one stroke

Children are to be deceived with
comfits and men with oaths

If you cut your oats green,
you get both king and queen

Comparisons are odious

The more laws, the more offenders

To offer much is a kind of denial

You cannot put an old head on young shoulders

He that would be old long, must be old betimes

Old shoes are easiest

Old wood is best to burn,
old horse to ride,
old books to read, and
old wine to drink

Old young, young old

Though old and wise, yet still advise

One master in a house is enough

In the country of the blind,
the one-eyed man is king

He that desires to make a market
of his ware, must watch an
opportunity to open his shop

The orange that is too hard squeezed
yields a bitter juice

Late children, early orphans

He who owes, is in all the wrong

Every man should take his own

A man must plough with
such oxen as he has

Obstinate oxen waste their strength

Once paid, never craved

It is more pain to do nothing than something

The inspecting officer's world smells of new paint

Every couple is not a pair

Content lodges oftener in the cottage
than in the palace

No man can guess in cold blood
what he may do in a passion

Serving one's own passions
is the greatest slavery

Change of pasture makes fat calves

Every path has a puddle

Patience is a flower that grows
not in every one's garden

Patience is a plaster for all sores

Patience is a virtue

Patience is the key of joy,
but haste is the key of sorrow

Patience provoked turns to fury

Patience surpasses learning

Patience under old injuries invites new ones

Patience with poverty is all a poor man's remedy

With the trowel of patience
we dig out the roots of truth

Patient men win the day

Better to pay and have little than
have much and be in debt

He that cannot pay, let him pray

Pay what you owe and
you'll know what you're worth

He who pays the piper calls the tune

Peace makes plenty

Where there is peace, God is

To live peaceably with all breeds good blood

The peacock has fair feathers, but foul feet

If you pay peanuts, you get monkeys

The old pearl-oyster produces a pearl

Plant pears for your heirs

You've got to eat a peck of dirt before you die

He who peeps through a hole,
may see what will vex him

The Peerage is the Englishman's Bible

Pen and ink is wit's plough

The pen is the tongue of the hand

Look after the pennies and
the pounds will look after themselves

A bad penny always turns up (again)

In for a penny, in for a pound

No penny, no pardon

Look after the pens and
the puns will take care of themselves

If the beginning is good,
the end must be perfect

One acre of performance is worth
twenty of the land of promise

There is nothing permanent except change

Perseverance kills the game

❀

It is not the beard that makes the philosopher

❀

Physician, heal thyself

❀

What can you expect from a pig but a grunt?

❀

Pigs may fly, but they are very unlikely birds

❀

The paleness of the pilot is the
strength of the storm

You can't fit a quart into a pint pot

Piss not against the wind

The pitcher that goes often
to the well is broken at last

You can drive out Nature with a pitchfork,
but she keeps on coming back

A little help is worth a deal of pity

A place for everything and everything in its place

All work and no play makes Jack a dull boy

He that would please all and himself too,
undertakes what he cannot do

You can't please everyone

Pleasing ware is half sold

Business before pleasure

Eat at pleasure, drink by measure

He that has plenty of goods shall have more

He who of plenty will take no heed, shall
find default in time of need

Plenty makes poor

A black plum is as sweet as a white

Thrifty is he whose pockets are
deep and arms short

A poet in adversity can hardly make verses

One man's meat is another man's poison

There can be no polish without abrasion

He is poor that God hates

Poor folks are glad of porridge

Poor men go to heaven as soon as rich

The poorer one is, the more devils one meets

Possession is nine points of the law

Possibilities are infinite

Don't spread the cloth till
the pot begins to boil

The pot calls the kettle black

To a boiling pot, flies come not

Beauty is potent but money is omnipotent

Bashfulness is an enemy to poverty

Be patient in poverty and
you may become rich

He that is in poverty, is still in suspicion

It is easier to commend poverty
than endure it

Laziness goes so slowly that
poverty overtakes it

Poverty and anger do not agree

Poverty and wealth are twin sisters

Poverty is an enemy to good manners

Poverty is no disgrace,
but is a great inconvenience

Poverty is not a shame,
but being ashamed of it is

Poverty is the mother of all arts

Slow rises worth by poverty depressed

When poverty comes in at the door,
love flies out of the window

Power tends to corrupt; and
absolute power corrupts absolutely

Knowledge is power

Mickle power makes many enemies

Practice makes perfect

A man's praise in his own mouth stinks

Praise by evil men is dispraise

Praise is a spur to the good,
a thorn to the evil

Praise is always pleasant

Praise is not pudding

271

Praise makes good men better,
and bad men worse

Praise none too much for all are fickle

Praise without profit puts little in the pot

Praise youth and it will prosper

They that value not praise, will never do
anything worthy of praise

True praise roots and spreads

Who praises St Peter does not blame St Paul

He praises who wishes to sell

He that praises himself, spatters himself

Absence sharpens love, presence strengthens it

He that fears you present will hate you absent

No time like the present

Present to the eye, present to the mind

Preserve the old, but know the new

Prettiness dies first

Prettiness makes no pottage

Prevention is better than cure

Heresy is the school of pride

It is not a sign of humility to
declaim against pride

Pride and grace dwelt never in one place

Pride and laziness would have
mickle upholding

Pride comes before a fall

Pride and poverty are ill met,
yet often seen together

Pride goes before, and shame follows after

Pride increases our enemies,
but puts our friends to flight

An ounce of mother is worth a ton of priest

Clothes make people, priests make brides

Women, priests, and poultry,
never have enough

Of a new prince, new bondage

He that puts on a public gown,
must put off a private person

A thousand probabilities do not make one truth

Others' problems are easy to solve

Procrastination is the thief of time

A man apt to promise is apt to forget

Promises are either broken or kept

Promises are like pie-crust, made to be broken

Promises may make friends,
but 'tis performance keeps them

A prophet is without honour in his own country

Prospect is often better than possession

Prosperity makes friends,
adversity tries them

A proud mind and a beggar's purse
agree not together

A proverb is the wit of one
and the wisdom of many

The proverb cannot be bettered

Though the proverb is abandoned,
it is not falsified

Proverbs are like butterflies,
some are caught, others fly away

Proverbs are the wisdom of the streets

Proverbs cannot be contradicted
(*Oh yes they can!*)

The genius, wit and spirit of a nation are
discovered in its proverbs

Provision in season makes a rich house

The proof of the pudding is in the eating

Puddings and paramours
should be hotly handled

A pullet in the pen is worth
a hundred in the fen

Punctuality is the politeness of princes

Punctuality is the soul of business

Like fault like punishment

Every sin brings its punishment with it

Look after the pens and the puns
will take care of themselves

A drunkard's purse is his bottle

An empty purse fills the face with wrinkles

An empty purse makes a full heart

He that has a full purse never wanted a friend

He that has no money needs no purse

The purse of the patient contracts the disease

Pursuits become habits

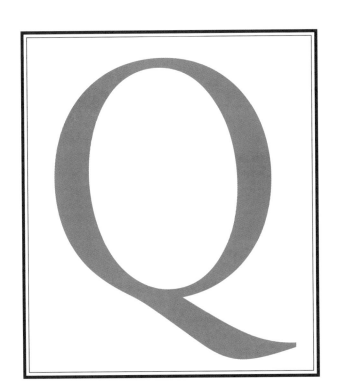

Give a loan and buy a quarrel

✾

You can't get a quart into a pint pot

✾

There's nowt so queer as folk

✾

It is not every question that
deserves an answer

✾

It is not every question that has an answer

Like question, like answer

Question for question is all fair

Ask no questions; be told no lies

He that nothing questions,
nothing learns

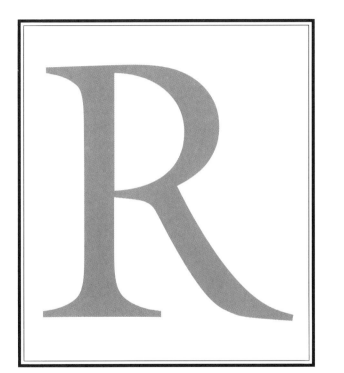

The race is got by running

The race is not to the swift,
nor the battle to the strong

A ragged colt may make a good horse

Bright rain makes fools fain

Rain before seven: fine before eleven

Rain from the east; wet two days at least

Rain, rain, go away, come again another day

The rain of tears is necessary
to the harvest of learning

It never rains but it pours

That thing which is rare is dear

Rats desert a sinking ship

'Because' is a woman's reason

Affection blinds reason

Reckless youth makes rueful age

The reckoning spoils the relish

Short reckonings make long friends

Evening red and morning grey
help the traveller on his way;
evening grey and morning red
bring down rain upon his head

Red sky in the morning
is the shepherd's warning;
Red sky at night is the shepherd's delight

Reek comes aye down again
however high it flees

The remedy for injuries is not to remember them

Marry in haste, repent at leisure

Anger begins with folly,
and ends with repentance

No reply is best

A change is as good as a rest

Never return to the restaurant
where you had that excellent meal

Quick returns make rich merchants

Revenge is sweet

Reward and punishment
are the walls of a city

Service without reward is punishment

A rich man can do nothing wrong

Be patient in poverty and you may become rich

He is not rich that possesses much,
but he that is content with what he has

He is rich enough that wants nothing

He that will be rich before night,
may be hanged before noon

He who has good health is young;
and he is rich who owes nothing

He who is content in his poverty,
is wonderfully rich

Poor by condition, rich by ambition

Rich men are stewards for the poor

Rich men may have what they will

The rich man has his ice in the summer,
the poor gets his in the winter

The rich man spends his money,
the poor man his strength

The rich man thinks of his future,
the poor man thinks of today

Children are poor men's riches

Gentility is but ancient riches

Riches alone make no man happy

Riches bring care and fears

From the sublime to the ridiculous
is but a step

Two wrongs don't make a right

Rome wasn't built in a day

Better sit still than rise and fall

He that rises late, must trot all day

He that rises not early,
never does a good day's work

In a great river, great fish are found;
but take heed lest you be drowned

Rivers need a spring

He keeps his road well enough
who gets rid of bad company

It's a long road that has no turning

Great boast, small roast

He that robs a scholar, robs twenty men

Who will not be ruled by the rudder,
must be ruled by the rock

The rod breaks no bones

All roads lead to Rome

It is ill sitting at Rome and
striving against the Pope

When in Rome do as the Romans do

Give a man enough rope and
he'll hang himself

A rose by any other name would smell sweet

No rose without a thorn

Money is round, and rolls away

It is royal to do right and receive abuse

There is no royal road to learning

Who will not be ruled by the rudder,
must be ruled by the rock

Better a civil denial than a rude grant

Better rue sit than rue flit

Many have been ruined by
buying good pennyworths

Rule youth well, and age will rule itself

He that has a fellow-ruler,
has an over-ruler

No man can be a good ruler,
unless he has first been ruled

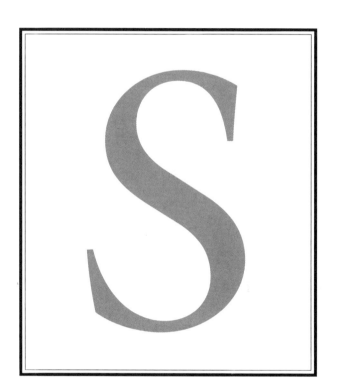

When the owl goes to the mouse picnic,
he's not there for the sack race

Easier said than done

Young saint, old devil

The best smell is bread, the best savour salt,
the best love that of children

The more it changes,
the more it remains the same

Make not your sauce before you
have caught the fish

Hear all, see all, and say nothing

Say as men say, but think to yourself

Doing is better than saying

A pitiful mother makes a scabby daughter

Science has no enemy but the ignorant

You scratch my back, and I'll scratch yours

Worse things happen at sea

A sieve will hold water better than a
woman's mouth a secret

Everything has its seed

Seeing is believing

Seek and ye shall find

Seek much, and get something;
seek little, and get nothing

Things are not always what they seem

Seldom seen, soon forgotten

Self-praise is no recommendation

Sell it cheap; buy it back dear

Separation secures manifest friendship

One must be a servant before one
can be a master

Saturday's servants never stay,
Sunday servants run away

Servants make the worst masters

Every fight has its shadow

Shame fades in the morning,
but debts remain from day to day

Shameful craving must have
shameful nay

Share and share alike

It is ill shaving against the wool

A leap year is never a good sheep year

One scabbed sheep will mar a whole flock

There's a black sheep in every family

He that burns most, shines most

Idleness is the shipwreck of chastity

No shoe fits every foot

Keep your shop and your shop
will keep you

Short folk are soon angry

The shortest answer is doing

Every man can rule a shrew
save he that has her

Shrouds have no pockets

There are two sides to every question

Out of sight, out of mind

Silence is a woman's best garment

Speech is silver, silence is golden

You can't make a silk purse out of a sow's ear

Ask a silly question and
you'll get a silly answer

No silver without its dross

When you go to buy, don't show your silver

White silver draws black lines

Every sin brings its punishment with it

Fear nothing but sin

It is no sin to sell dear,
but a sin to give ill measure

Sin is the root of sorrow

The wages of sin is death

To fall into sin is human,
to remain in sin is devilish

Learn to say before you sing

The greater the sinner the greater the saint

Old sins cast long shadows

Better sit still than rise and fall

Six feet of earth make all men equal

Don't sell the skin till you
have caught the bear

If the sky falls we shall catch larks

Slander leaves a score behind it

The slanderer kills a thousand times,
the assassin but once

Lean liberty is better than fat slavery

Let not a child sleep upon bones

It is good sleeping in a whole skin

He who sleeps all the morning,
may go a begging all the day after

If the laird slight the lady,
so will all the kitchen boys

There's many a slip 'twixt cup and lip

Sloth, like rust, consumes
faster than labour wears

For the diligent the week has seven todays;
for the slothful seven tomorrows

The slothful man is the beggar's brother

Slow but sure wins the race

A sluggard takes an hundred steps because he would not take one in due time

The sluggard's convenient season never comes

Every day is a holiday for the sluggard

It's a small world

Small birds must yet have meat

Small is beautiful

There's no smoke without fire

Deflect not that snail;
he may be going to the bank

Tramp on a snail and she'll shoot out her horns

Women are the snares of Satan

A snow year, a rich year

What soberness conceals,
drunkenness reveals

Sod's Law decrees
That the cure is worse than the disease

A son is a son till he gets him a wife,
but a daughter's a daughter
all the days of her life

Soon ripe, soon rotten

322

Sooner begun, sooner done

An hundred pounds of sorrow pays
not one ounce of debt

Better fat sorrow than lean

Sorrow is soon enough when it come

Sorrow will pay no debt

He that goes a borrowing, goes a sorrowing

You reap what you sow

You can't make a silk purse out of a sow's ear

Spare when you're young,
and spend when you're old

Better a sparrow in the hand than
a pigeon on the roof

Women and sparrows twitter in company

Speak and speed, ask and have

Speak when you're spoken to

More haste, less speed

Who spends before he thrives,
will beg before he thinks

The spirit is willing but the flesh is weak

He that sups with the devil needs
a long spoon

A leopard cannot change his spots

There are spots even in the sun

Throw out a sprat to catch a mackerel

Don't shut the stable door
after the horse has bolted

An army of stags led by a lion would
be more formidable than one
of lions led by a stag

He stands not surely that never slips

He that stays in the valley,
shall never get over the hill

If you steal for others you shall
be hanged yourself

Steer not after every mariner's direction

The first step is the hardest

The greatest step is that out of doors

A straight stick is crooked in the water

Sticks and stones may break my bones
but names will never hurt me

He that will not go over the stile
must be thrust through the gate

Still waters run deep

After your fling, watch for the sting

He that steals honey should be aware
of the sting

Bees that have honey in their mouths
have stings in their tails

He who squeezes in between the onion
and the peel, picks up its stink

No man cries stinking fish

Stolen waters are sweet

An army marches on its stomach

A rolling stone gathers no moss

Constant dripping wears away the stone

Though stones were changed to gold,
the heart of man would not be satisfied

Between two stools you fall to the ground

After a storm comes a calm

Straight trees have crooked roots

A drowning man ill clutches at a straw

A man of straw is worth a woman of gold

It's the last straw that breaks the camel's back

It is ill striving against the stream

It is in the garden of patience
that strength grows best

❀

Wisdom is better than strength

❀

Strike while the iron's hot

❀

Little strokes fell great oaks

❀

St Swithin's day, if thou dost rain,
for forty days it will remain

A man's studies pass into his character

Stuffing holds out storm

A stumble may prevent a fall

Don't build the sty before the litter comes

The subject's love is the king's lifeguard

From the sublime to the
ridiculous is but a step

Suffer the ill and look for the good

Sufficient unto the day is the evil thereof

The last suitor wins the maid

Don't let the sun go down on your anger

If the sun goes pale to bed,
'twill rain tomorrow, it is said

If wind follow the sun's course,
expect fair weather

No sun without a shadow

There's nothing new under the sun

I am a sundial, and I make a botch,
Of what is done far better by a watch

What is the good of a sundial
in the shade?

After dinner sit awhile,
after supper walk a mile

Better to go to bed supperless
than to rise in debt

He sups ill who eats all at dinner

One swallow doesn't make a summer

If every man would sweep before his own
door, the city would soon be clean

Home, sweet home

Sweet appears sour when we pay

336

Sweet are the uses of adversity

Sweet meat will have sour sauce

Who swims in sin shall sink in sorrow

Don't cast your pearls before swine

What you loose on the swings
you gain on the roundabouts

He who lives by the sword dies by the sword

It is ill putting a sword in a madman's hand

Learning in the breast of a bad man
is as a sword in the hand of a madman

The pen is mightier than the sword

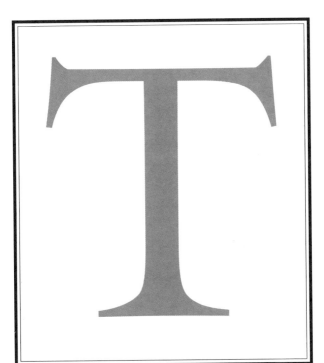

Tailors and writers must mind the fashion

Take things as they come

Talk is but talk; but 'tis money buys land

Women are great talkers

Don't spoil the ship for a hap'orth of tar

Every one to his taste

You can't teach an old dog new tricks

A teaspoon of petrol is enough to wreck a car

He that is busy, is tempted by but one devil;
he that is idle, by a legion

A kindness forced deserves no thanks

He loses his thanks who promises and delays

Old thanks pay not for a new debt

A thief passes for a gentleman
when stealing has made him rich

Hang a thief when he's young,
and he'll not steal when he's old

He that brings up his son to nothing,
breeds a thief

Set a thief to catch a thief

The thief doth fear each bush an officer

All are not thieves that dogs bark at

Little thieves are hanged,
but great ones escape

There is honour among thieves

Thieves and rogues have the best luck,
if they do but 'scape hanging

One thing at a time, and that done well,
is a very good thing, as many can tell

Thinking is very far from knowing

He who is master of his thirst
is master of his health

He that goes to bed thirsty, rises healthy

Beware of an oak, it draws the stroke;
avoid an ash, it counts the lash;
creep under a thorn,
it can save you from harm

If you lie upon thorns when young,
you'll lie upon thorns when old

He who holds the thread holds the ball

He that will thrive, must rise at five;
he that has thriven, may lie till seven;
but he that will never thrive
may lie till eleven

A quiet conscience sleeps in thunder

Thursday come and the week is gone

He who rides a tiger is afraid to dismount

If you do not enter a tiger's den,
you cannot get his cubs

A tightrope is the same whether an inch
or a mile from the ground

A stitch in time saves nine

Tempus fugit (Time flies)

There's a time for everything

Those that make the best use of their
time have none to spare

Time and tide wait for no man

Time is a great healer

Time lost cannot be recalled

Time passes away, but sayings remain

Time, not the mind, puts an end to love

Work expands to fill the time available

Times change and we with them

If ifs and ands were pots and pans,
there'd be no trade for tinkers

Never put off till tomorrow
what you can do today

One today is worth two tomorrows

Tomorrow is another day

Tomorrow never comes

A long tongue is a sign of a short hand

A still tongue makes a wise head

An eye for an eye, and a tooth for a tooth

There's always room at the top

A strong town is not won in an hour

The town for wealth, the country for health

There was never a good town
but had a mire at one end of it

Jack of all trades is master of none

Every up train's got to be a down
train sometime

It is better to travel hopefully than to arrive

Travellers change climates, not conditions

Though an ass goes a-travelling,
he'll not come home a horse

He that travels far, knows much

Learning is a treasure which
accompanies its owner everywhere

Treat not but with principals

As the twig is bent, so is the tree inclined

He that loves the tree, loves the branch

He that plants a tree plants for prosperity

He who aims at the moon may hit the top
of a tree; he who aims at the top of a tree
is unlikely to get off the ground

There is no tree but bears some fruit

Do not triumph before the victory

A trouble shared is a trouble halved

Never trouble trouble
till trouble troubles you

Don't meet troubles halfway

Newer is truer

Trust is dead, ill payment killed it

Trust is the mother of deceit

Trust not a new friend nor an old enemy

Trust not a woman when she weeps

A thousand probabilities
do not make one truth

Better a lie that heals
than a truth that wounds

Speak the truth and shame the devil

Truth has a good face, but bad clothes

Truth is stranger than fiction

You never know what you can do till you try

There's many a good tune played on
an old fiddle

With twenty-six soldiers of lead,
we will conquer the world

No man can do two
things at once

Better unborn than unbred

Come not to counsel uncalled

If my aunt had been a man,
she'd have been my uncle

When two meet on uncommon ground,
a hidden friendship may be found

The unexpected always happens

An unhappy man's cart is eith to tumble

United we stand, divided we fall

Unminded, unmoaned

Unpaid debts are unforgiven sins

Unseen, unrued

Better untaught than ill taught

To speak of a usurer at the table mars the wine

Usurers are always good husbands

Usurers live by the fall of heirs, as swine
by the dropping of acorns

Usury is murder

A valiant man's look is more than
a coward's sword

❀

Beauty's sister is vanity, and her daughter lust

❀

An ounce of vanity spoils a
hundredweight of merit

❀

Variety is the spice of life

❀

An ape's an ape, a varlet's a varlet,
though they be clad in silk or scarlet

Empty vessels make the most noise

One hates not the person, but the vice

Vice is its own punishment,
and sometimes its own cure

Vice is often clothed in virtue's habit

Where vice is, vengeance follows

Do not triumph before the victory

366

He gets a double victory,
who conquers himself

It is a great victory that comes without blood

The vine brings forth three grapes:
the first of pleasure,
the second of drunkenness,
the third of sorrow

Nothing that is violent is permanent

A fair woman without virtue is like palled wine

Adversity is the touchstone of virtue

Love is the touchstone of virtue

Of money, wit, and virtue, believe
one-fourth of what you hear

The virtue of a coward is suspicion

Virtue flies from the heart of
a mercenary man

Virtue is its own reward

Virtue is the only true nobility

Who that in youth no virtue uses,
in age all honour him refuses

Wisdom and virtue are like the
two wheels of a cart

One volunteer is worth two pressed men

Vows made in storms are
forgotten in calms

That voyage never has
luck where each
one has a vote

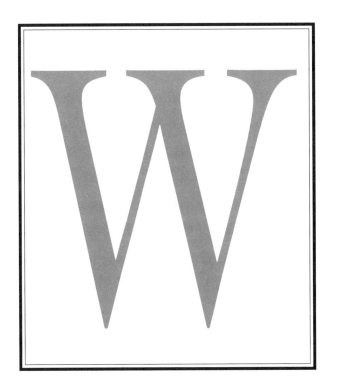

He that serves well need not ask his wages

Everything comes to him who waits

If they've got you by the wallet,
they've got you by the short and curlies

Walls have ears

He who plants a walnut tree,
expects not to eat of the fruit

Wanton kittens make sober cats

He that has it and will not keep it;
he that wants it and will not seek it;
he that drinks and is not dry,
shall want money as well as I

A just war is better than an unjust peace

Clothe thee in war: arm thee in peace

If you want peace, you must prepare for war

Many may begin a war, few can end it

War is death's feast

War is sweet to them that know it not

Ill ware is never cheap

He was slain that had warning,
not he that took it

He that is not in the wars is not out of danger

Wars brings scars

For washing his hands,
none sells his lands

Waste not, want not

A watched pot never boils

Blood is thicker than water

Don't go near the water
till you learn how to swim

You never miss the water till the well runs dry

❀

Soft wax will take any impression

❀

Weak men had need be witty

❀

A man's wealth is his enemy

❀

He that marries for wealth, sells his liberty

❀

Knowledge makes one laugh,
but wealth makes one dance

Little wealth, little care

✽

Men get wealth and women keep it

✽

The greatest wealth is contentment with a little

✽

Wealth is best known by want

✽

Wealth is the test of a man's character

✽

Where wealth is established, it is difficult
for friendship to find a place

Wine and wealth change wise men's manners

Worth has been underrated,
ever since wealth has been overrated

A man of courage never wants weapons

All the weapons of war will not arm fear

Weapons breed peace

It is better to wear out than to rust out

Oh, what a tangled web we weave,
when first we practice to deceive!

No garden without its weeds

The weeds overgrow the corn

Weeds want no sowing

Learn weeping and you shall gain laughing

Weight and measure take away strife

All's well that ends well

He that lives well is learned enough

That which is well done is twice done

A well-bred youth neither speaks of himself
nor, being spoken to, remains silent

There's nowt so wenge as other's dreams

Every why has a wherefore

Where there is whispering there is lying

The filth under the white snow
the sun discovers

Two blacks don't make a white

I am a white-noise generator, and I make a balls,
Of what is done far better by the Niagara Falls

He that lives wickedly can hardly die honestly

He that has no wife, beats her oft

Need makes the old wife trot

There is one good wife in the country,
and every man thinks he has her

Who has a fair wife needs more than two eyes

Where there's a will there's a way

Where your will is ready, your feet are light

Will buys and money pays

Will is the cause of woe

Nothing is impossible to a willing heart

Willows are weak yet they bind other wood

Corn is cleansed with wind,
and the soul with chastenings

If wind follow the sun's course,
expect fair weather

The north wind does blow,
and we shall have snow

The wind in one's face makes one wise

Drink wine in winter for cold,
and in summer for heat

Good wine engenders good blood

Good wine needs no bush

The wine is the master,
the goodness is the butler's

❀

When the wine is in, the wit is out

❀

When wine sinks, words swim

❀

Wine and wealth change wise men's manners

❀

Wine and youth increase love

❀

Wine is the glass of the mind

Wine makes all sorts of creatures at table

You can't put new wine into old bottles

You cannot know the wine by the barrel

Winter's thunder and summer's flood
never boded Englishman good

Winter's thunder makes old man's wonder

Anger restrained is wisdom gained

Experience is the mother of wisdom

He who wisdom has at will,
an angry heart can hold him still

It is wit to pick a lock and steal a horse,
but wisdom to let them alone

Trouble brings experience
and experience brings wisdom

Wisdom and virtue are like the
two wheels of a cart

Wisdom is neither inheritance nor legacy

Wisdom is the least burdensome travelling pack

Without wisdom, wealth is worthless

A fool may give a wise man counsel

A wise man sometimes changes his mind,
a fool never

A wise man esteems every place
to be his own country

A wise man is never less alone
than when he is alone

Adversity makes a man wise, not rich

He is wise enough that can keep
himself warm

He is wise that is honest

He that is truly wise and great,
lives both too early and too late

He that is wise by day is no fool by night

No man can play the fool so well as
the wise man

No man is born wise or learned

No man so wise but he may be deceived

The wise seek wisdom, a fool has found it

Wise is the man that has two loaves,
and sells one to buy a lily

Wise men have their mouth in their heart,
fools have their heart in their mouth

Better to have than to wish

Wishers and woulders be no
good householders

If wishes were horses, beggars would ride

Wishes can never fill a sack

A man may learn wit every day

But a little wit will serve a fortunate man

❀

Wit without learning is like a tree without fruit

❀

Wood in a wilderness, moss on a mountain,
and wit in a poor man's breast,
are little thought of

❀

Conscience is a thousand witnesses

❀

Bachelors' wives and maids'
children are well taught

In wiving and thriving a man should
take counsel of all the world

Woe's to them that have the cat's dish,
and she aye mewing

Woes unite foes

A thief knows a thief as a wolf knows a wolf

He that makes himself a sheep
shall be eaten by the wolf

The death of a young wolf never
comes too soon

The wolf may lose his teeth,
but never his nature

Who keeps company with the
wolf will learn to howl

The death of the wolves is
the safety of the sheep

A man is as old as he feels,
and a woman as old as she looks

A bad woman is worse than a bad man

A fair woman without virtue
is like palled wine

A man is as old as the woman he feels

A woman and a cherry are
painted for their own harm

A woman conceals what she knows not.

A woman either loves or hates in extremes

A woman has an eye more than a man

❀

A woman is as old as the man she feels

❀

A woman kissed is half won

❀

A woman's sword is her tongue,
and she does not let it rust

Hell hath no fury like a woman scorned

Who has a woman has an eel by the tail

Woeful is the household that wants a woman

All women are good

Choose neither women nor linen
by candlelight

Forbid a thing, and that women will do

The more women look in their glass,
the less they look to their house

Three women make a market

Women and dogs set men together by the ears

Women and music should never be dated

Women and sparrows twitter in company

Women in state affairs are like
monkeys in glass-shops

Women laugh when they can,
and weep when they will

Women may blush to hear what
they were not ashamed to do

Women must have their wills
when they live, because
they make none when they die

Women resist in order to be conquered

Women will have the last word

Women's counsel is cold

Women's instinct is often truer than
men's reasoning

Wonder is the daughter of ignorance

To woo is a pleasure in a young man,
a fault in an old

A little wood will heat a little oven

Do not halloo till you are out of the wood

He that woos a maid,
must seldom come in her sight;
but he that woos a widow must woo
her day and night

A man that breaks his word,
bids others be false to him

One ill word asks another

Children pick up words as pigeons
do peas, and utter them again as
God shall please

Deeds are males; words are females

Good words anoint us,
and ill do unjoint us

Words are but wind

Words are mere bubbles of water
but deeds are drops of gold

Words fly, writings remain

A woman's work is never done

All work and no play makes Jack a dull boy

If you won't work, you shan't eat

Mix work with leisure
and you will never go mad

The end crowns the work

Work expands to fill the time available

A bad workman blames his tools

Better be out of the world than
out of the fashion

Half the world doesn't know
how the other half lives

It is a good world,
but they are ill that are on it

It takes all sorts to make a world

The world is a net, the more we stir in it,
the more we are entangled

The world is a stage and every
man plays his part

❀

The world is bound to no man

❀

The world still he keeps at his staff's end that
needs not to borrow and never will lend

❀

The world will not last alway

❀

Even a worm will turn

❀

It's a short worm that has no turning

The early bird catches the worm

If you see a town worshipping a calf,
grass and feed him

A man's worth is the worth of his land

Slow rises worth by poverty depressed

The worth of a thing is what it will bring

A soft answer turneth away wrath

When wrath speaks, wisdom veils her face

Tailors and writers must mind the fashion

Writing destroys the memory

Do wrong once and you shall never
hear the end of it

No wrong without a remedy

Wrong never comes right

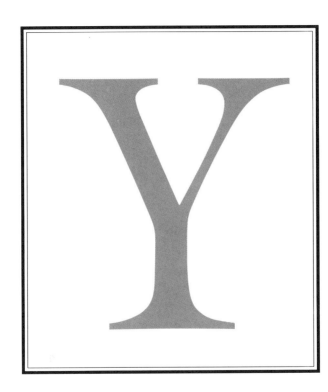

A cherry year, a merry year; a plum year,
a dumb year; a pear year, a dear year

Whom the gods love dies young

A growing youth has a wolf in his belly

If youth knew what age would crave,
it would both get and save

Wine and youth increase love

Youth and white paper take any impression

Youth never casts for peril

Yule is young in Yule even,
and as old in Saint Stephen

A good yule makes a fat churchyard

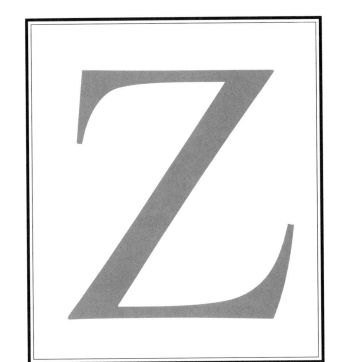

Zeal without knowledge is a
runaway horse

Zeal is fit only for wise men, but is
found mostly in fools

This edition first published in 2003 by
Book Blocks an imprint of CRW Publishing Limited
69 Gloucester Crescent, London NW1 7EG

❊

ISBN 1 904633 16 1

❊

Text arrangement and Introduction
© Rodney A. M. Dale 2003

❊

❊

The compiler thanks Charlotte Edwards,
who assembled and sorted vast quantities of
gnomic utterances for evaluation and selection,
and Antony Gray, who designed the
collection into beauteous reality.

Typeset in Great Britain by Antony Gray
Printed and bound in China

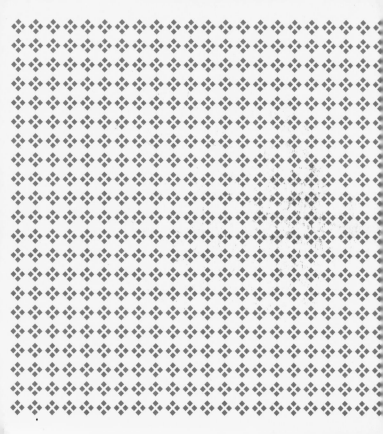